1 Sieh dir die folgende Seite einmal genau an. Kannst du die Wörter in Gruppen einteilen? Unterstreiche mit verschiedenen Farben.

1. Gruppe: Essen und Trinken / food and drink
2. Gruppe: Kosmetik und Kleider / cosmetics and clothes
3. Gruppe: Musik, Sport und Hobbys / music, sports and hobbies

Ergänze auch Wörter, die du außerdem kennst.

Drink
Light
Fast Food
Tennis
Skateboard
Tonic
Telefon-Modem
Skiing
Haar-Styling
Popstar
Orange
Shampoo
Sommer-T-Shirts
Gameboy
Baseball cap
A star is born:
Fitness-Kleidung
Käse-Sandwich
Ketchup
Inline skating
It's "Tea Time"
Eyeliner
Snack
Made in England
COMPUTER-TISCH

2   My English words

Schneide selbst Wörter aus und stelle
ein Plakat her mit der Überschrift:

♡ J like ♡

Was du auch tun kannst:
Binde dein Englischheft mit einem
selbstgemachten Einband ein.
Dafür klebst du die englischen
Wörter, die du gefunden hast,
auf ein DIN-A3-Zeichenblatt.
Du kannst es auch noch mit
durchsichtiger Klebefolie überziehen.

**3   Lies den folgenden Text.
Du kennst noch nicht alle Wörter, aber schon sehr viele.
Unterstreiche alle Wörter, die du kennst.**

English is no problem!

Hello everybody! My name is Susan. I am eleven.
I have a brother, Jack. He is a clown, but a clever clown.
We live in London, in Great Britain. I speak English, of course.
I have a dog, a hamster and three goldfish. The goldfish live
in an aquarium. The hamster has a house, a shoe box in a
cage. My hamster likes popcorn, and I like popcorn, too.
I love cornflakes in the morning, and I often eat a grapefruit
or toast. I drink tea. I love steak or chicken for Sunday dinner
and then ice-cream – mmm! My favourite drink is lemonade.
My mother says milk is better for me – ugh, I am not a baby!
Do you like music? I like pop music, rock, and country
music – I have 50 or 60 CDs. I am a Sabrina fan. I have her
poster in my room. There is a music festival in London this
summer. My mother says I can go there.

a) Zähle doch einmal, wie viele Wörter du schon kennst. Wie viele Wörter sind es?

b) Hör dir jetzt den Text von Cassette/CD an. Hast du noch mehr Wörter erkannt?
Unterstreiche sie auch.

Ich kenne schon _____ englische Wörter.

4 An easy puzzle

Suche die englischen Wörter und umrahme sie.
Die Buchstaben können in folgenden Richtungen stehen:

B	T	S	H	E	R	I	F	F	R	B	T
A	O	L	P	U	L	L	O	V	E	R	E
B	A	D	P	S	T	O	O	B	T	A	K
Y	S	O	Y	R	U	T	T	O	U	T	R
S	T	E	I	B	R	J	B	X	P	S	A
I	H	H	P	A	U	G	A	C	M	M	M
T	S	O	I	U	N	I	L	E	O	L	R
T	E	N	R	I	E	O	L	P	C	I	E
E	E	A	P	T	W	K	E	D	O	F	P
R	A	M	M	N	S	N	A	D	I	H	U
S	A	G	E	N	T	L	E	M	A	N	S
C	K	E	T	C	H	U	P	O	P	M	G

baby-sitter ✓   filmstar   pop   team
body-building   football   pullover   toast
boots   top
box   gentleman   sheriff   trainer
                                   shop   T-shirt
camping   ketchup   shorts
clown   supermarket
computer   made
                 make-up

9 Buchstaben bleiben übrig, sie ergeben ein Kleidungsstück.

1

A1 Wer sitzt hier in der Snackbar (von links nach rechts)?

1 This is _____

2 _____

3 _____

4 That is _____

5 _____

6 _____

A2 a) Wie heißen diese drei Fragen richtig?

your – what's – name   _____ ?

from – are – where – you   _____ ?

a coke – about – what   _____ ?

b) Ergänze die Fragen in diesem Gespräch:

Charlie: Hi, I'm Charlie. _____ name?

Karim: My name is Karim.

Charlie: Where _____, Karim?

Karim: From Notting Hill. _____ from?

Charlie: I'm from Hendon. _____ a drink?

Karim: Yes, good idea.

A3 **Frage deine Klassenkameraden:**

1. What's your name?
2. Where are you from?

Schreibe die Antworten hier auf.

name: from:

1 _____
2 _____
3 _____
4 _____
5 _____
6 _____

Jetzt stelle sie anderen Klassenkameraden vor:

Hello, this is Miriam. She's from Dortmund.
This is Marco. He's from …

B 1 a) Ordne die Wörter diesen Bildern zu.

1. lake   2. park   3. river   4. road

_____   _____   _____   _____

b) Benutze diese Wörter, um etwas über deinen Wohnort zu sagen.

_____ park

_____ river

_____ is a lake   in _____

_____ road

B 2

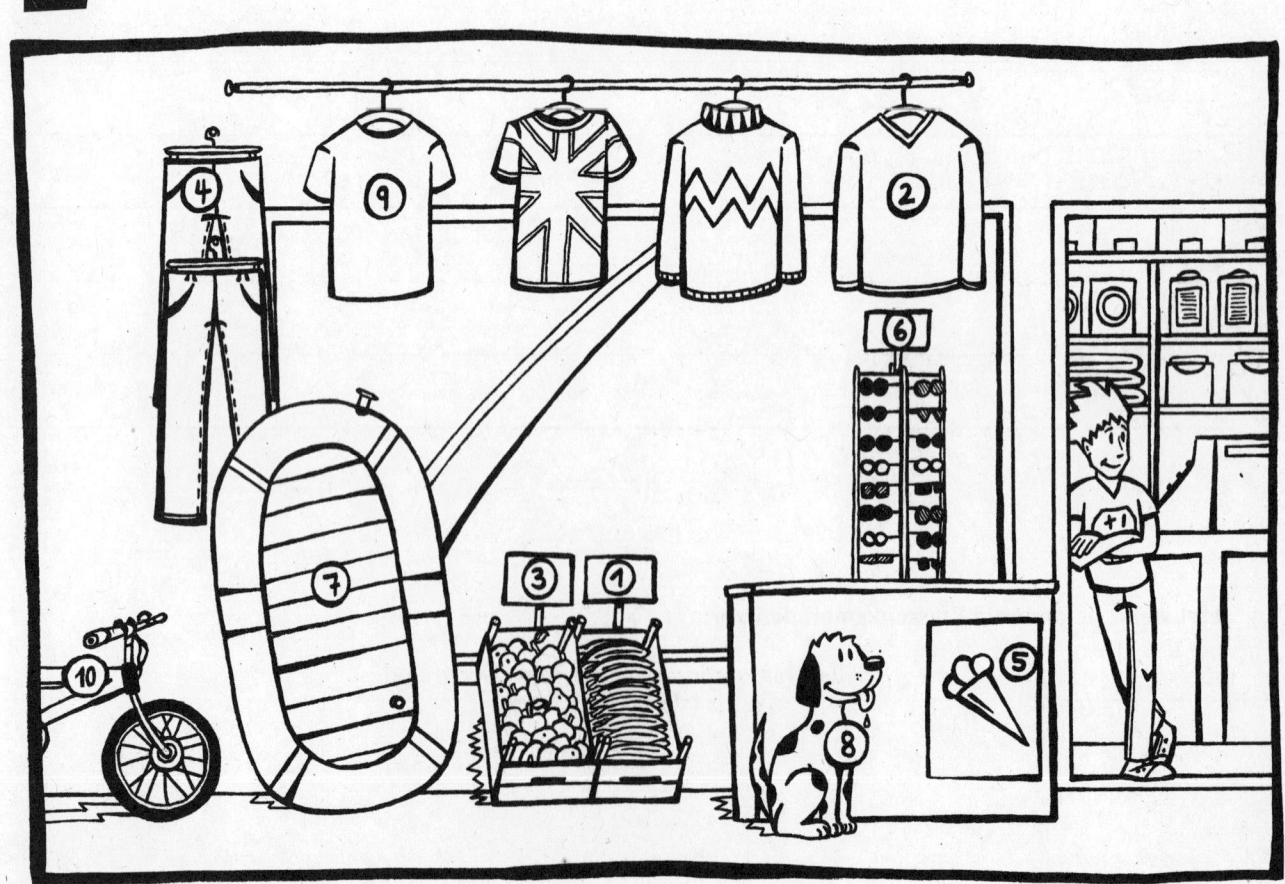

a) **Finde die Wörter für die Gegenstände Nr. 2 – 10 im Bild.
Wie heißt das Lösungswort?**

1 b a n a n a s

2 _ _ _ _ _

3 _ _ _ _ _

4 _ _ _ _

5 _ _ _ - _ _ _

6 _ _ _ _ _ _ _ _

7 _ _ _ _ _ _

8 _ _ _ _

9 _ _ - _ _ _ _

10 _ _ _ _

b) **Wo sind die Dinge vor dem Geschäft?**

⬅ on the left   in the middle   on the right ➡

The bananas are in the middle.

B3 Wie heißen die Farben?

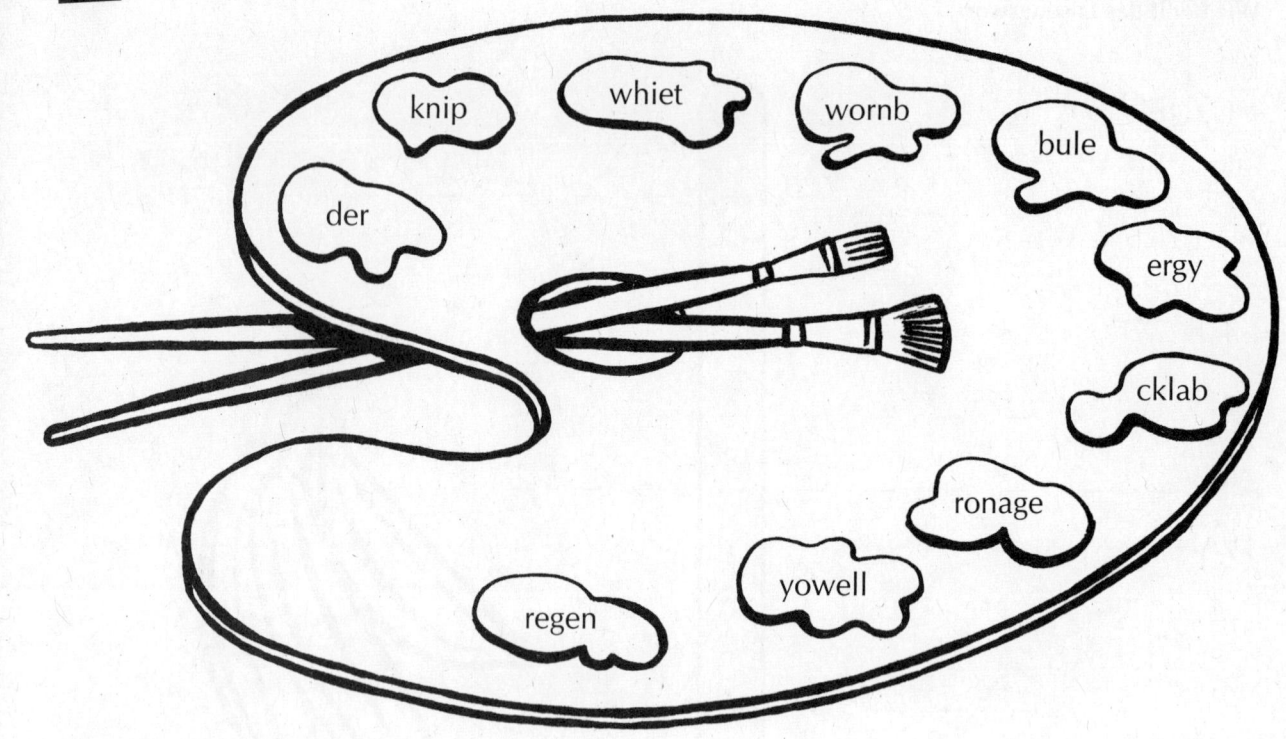

- knip
- whiet
- wornb
- bule
- der
- ergy
- cklab
- ronage
- yowell
- regen

Schreibe die Farben richtig auf und male die Farbkleckse aus.

_____

_____

B4 Wer trägt was? Sieh in dein Textbook auf S. 8 und mache ein Plus bei den Personen, die so ein Kleidungsstück tragen.

	Gillian	Susan	Karim	Charlie
orange pullover				
brown jeans				
green T-shirt				
red jacket				
black skirt		+		
yellow jacket				
blue jeans				

Vergleiche deine Ergebnisse dann mit deinem Nachbarn:
Susan is the girl in the black skirt.
Karim is the boy in the ...

B5 Kannst du die folgenden Wörter unter die richtigen Bilder schreiben?

> she   her   a girl   its name   a boy   its   it
> her pullover   his   he   his name   her name   a dog   its colour   his jeans

_____   _____   _____
_____   _____   _____
_____   _____   _____
_____   _____   _____
_____   _____   _____

B6 Schreibe die Wörter richtig in die Lücken.

> he – my – you – I – she – his – its – her – it – your

My name is Emma. _____ am from London. _____ bike is green and yellow.

Vera is an English girl. _____ is from Hendon. _____ friend Gillian is from Notting Hill.

Charlie is an English boy. _____ is from Hendon, too. _____ favourite colour is grey.

There is a dog in front of the Superstore. _____ name is Kenny. _____ is David's dog.

Are _____ from Notting Hill? Is Gillian _____ friend?

And YOU? _____ name is _____. ___ am from _____.

C1 Was ist in dieser Schultasche?

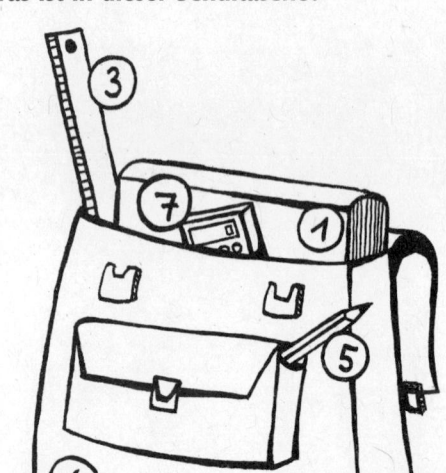

1 _____
2 _____
3 _____
4 _____
5 _____
6 _____
7 _____

C2 Sieh dir das Bild an.
Ergänze in den folgenden Sätzen in, on, at.

1 Vera, David and Charlie are _____ the classroom.

2 David is _____ the window.

3 Charlie is _____ his desk.

4 The sandwich is _____ the pencil case.

5 The teacher is _____ the door.

6 The books are _____ the schoolbag.

7 One chair is_____ the desk.

8 The calculator is _____ the chair.

C3 Schreibe acht Sätze über dein Klassenzimmer.

Claudia/ Jens /…		at the top		the picture
The calculator		on the left		the desk
	is			
The teacher		in the middle	of	the classroom
	are			
My pencils		on the right		Andreas/…
…		at the bottom		…

C 4 Was sagst du auf Englisch, wenn …

1 … du jemanden nicht verstanden hast?
2 … du dir von deiner/m Nachbarn/in einen Bleistift leihen willst?
3 … du nicht weißt, was „Lehrerin" auf Englisch heißt?
4 … du nicht weißt, was *eraser* auf Deutsch heißt?
5 … du deine/n Nachbarn/in fragen willst, ob er/sie dein Federmäppchen hat?

a) Can I have your pencil, please?
b) What is the German word for "eraser"?
c) Can you say that again, please?
d) What is the English word for "Lehrerin"?
e) Do you have my pencil case?

Schreibe die Buchstaben hier hinein:

1	2	3	4	5

C 5 Schreibe die Zahlwörter im Kreuzworträtsel auf Englisch.

C 6 Schreibe acht Sätze zu deinen Lieblingspersonen oder deinen Lieblingsgegenständen.

My favourite | colour
singer
sportsperson
food
drink
group
song
film
book/comic
club | is …

1 _____
2 _____
3 _____
4 _____
5 _____
6 _____
7 _____
8 _____

Detective page

D1 Schau dir Seite 15 bis 19 in deinem Textbook an und sammle Wörter mit

wh... _____

...oo... _____

...ou... _____

...th... _____

...ea... _____

D2 Suche dir aus Theme 1 eine Person aus und schreibe in Englisch alles auf, was du schon über sie weißt.

D3 Suche auf Seite 19 in deinem Textbook acht Wörter heraus.
Mach daraus ein Rätsel für deine/n Partner/in, indem du die Buchstaben durcheinanderbringst, z. B.
books – kobos.

D4 Wie viele Wörter findest du zu diesem Begriff?

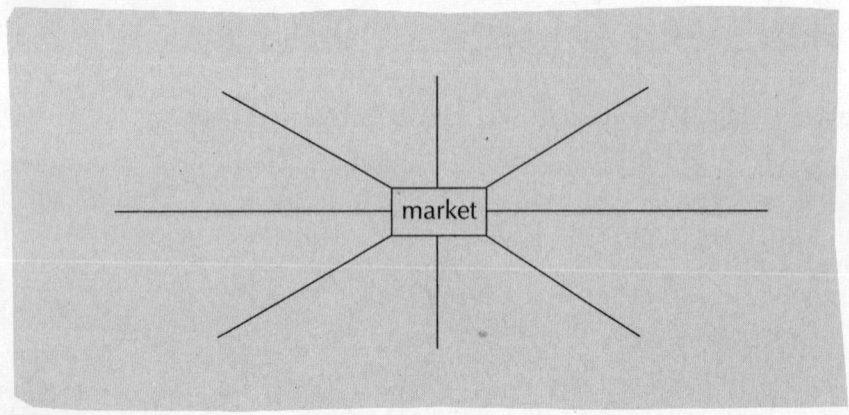

market

D5 Es heißt: **a** pen, **aber** **an** orange pen,
 a banana, **an** apple

Sieh dir Theme 1 noch einmal an und suche fünf weitere Beispiele für a/an.

D6 Schreibe zehn englische Wörter auf, die du besonders wichtig findest.

A1

Sieh dir Text und Bilder auf Seite 24 im Textbook an.
Ergänze in den folgenden Sätzen diese Wörter:
– „is" oder „are" und
– „in", „in front of" und „behind".

Beispiel: ... Mrs Williams ... the bathroom?
Is Mrs Williams in the bathroom?

1 _____ David _____ the bathroom?
2 David and his mother _____ not _____ the classroom.
3 His mother _____ not _____ the bathroom.
4 Mrs Williams _____ not _____ the mirror.
5 David _____ not _____ the door.
6 _____ David _____ the mirror?
7 It _____ eight o'clock and David _____ not ready.

A2

Finde die Wörter für die Körperteile und schreibe sie an die richtige Stelle.
Mit einem Spiegel kannst du deine Lösungen prüfen.

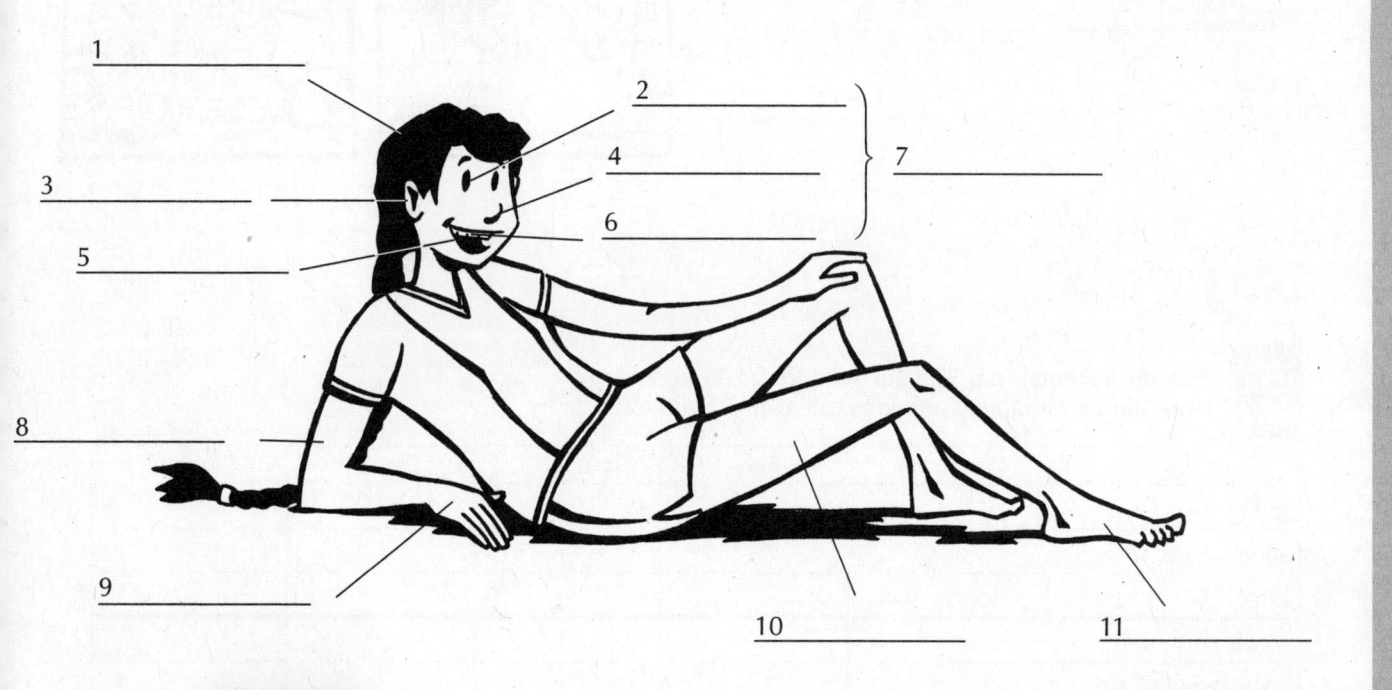

1 _____
2 _____
3 _____
4 _____
5 _____
6 _____
7 _____
8 _____
9 _____
10 _____
11 _____

hair, head, ear, arm, leg, nose, foot, teeth, eye, mouth, hand

A3 Wo tut es weh? Sieh dir die Bilder an und finde die richtigen Wörter.

Ow! My teeth!

1 Ow! My _____!
2 Ow! My _____!
3 Ow! _____!
4 Ow! _____!
5 _____!
6 _____!
7 _____!
8 _____!

A4 Sieh dir nochmals das Bild auf Seite 26 im Textbook an. Höre die Beschreibung und kreuze entsprechend an:

	Mr Smith	Miss Tate	Mrs Sinclair	Mr Carlucci
tall				
short				
big				
black curly hair				
long straight hair				
short black hair				
blonde hair				
black jacket and brown trousers				
dark green skirt and light green T-shirt				
brown jacket and blue jeans				
blue raincoat				

A5 Male einen Clown und beschreibe ihn dann deiner Nachbarin / deinem Nachbarn. Kann sie/er deinen Clown zeichnen?

> My clown is short.
> His nose is red.
> His ears are ...

A6 Höre dir diese Geschichte an und male ein Bild von Bobby.

2

B1 a) Sieh dir die Bilder und den Text auf Seite 28 im Textbook an.
Kreuze an, was Gillian und ihre Mutter frühstücken.

1	toast	☐	7	marmalade	☐
2	baked beans	☐	8	eggs	☐
3	milk	☐	9	coffee	☐
4	sausages	☐	10	tea	☐
5	sugar	☐	11	cornflakes	☐
6	butter	☐	12	bacon	☐

b) Sieh dir nochmals alle Wörter an und sage, welche davon zusammenpassen.

B2 Finde heraus, wie diese Sätze richtig heißen und wer sie sagt, Mrs Collins oder Gillian:

1 you – up – are: *Mrs Collins:* _____?

2 milk – on – the – is – table – the: _____?

3 I – can – baked beans – too – have:

_____?

4 ready – breakfast – is – come on:

_____.

5 marmalade – the – cupboard – the – is – in – still:

_____.

6 late – work – I'm – for: _____.

B3

a) Mithilfe des Bildes kannst du herausfinden, was Davids Lieblingsfrühstück ist.

Lösung:
David likes hot _____.

b) Denke dir ein Rätsel für deine Nachbarin / deinen Nachbarn aus: Was ist DEIN Lieblingsfrühstück?

B4 Befrage deine Klassenkameraden, wie ihr Sonntagsfrühstück aussieht.
Bildet Gruppen von etwa 6 Personen und tragt euch in den Fragebogen ein:

NAME	TIME	PLACE	DRINK	FOOD

Kannst du den Fragebogen auch auswerten? Benutze diese Sätze und schreibe in dein Heft:

_____ boys and girls have breakfast at _____.
_____ boys and girls have _____ in the
_____.
_____ boys and girls have _____ for breakfast.
Only one girl/boy has _____.

B5 Hier fehlen Zahlen! Kannst du sie richtig eintragen?

1 four – _____ – six
2 twelve – _____ – fourteen
3 seventeen – _____ – nineteen
4 ten, twenty – _____ – forty
5 twenty-one – _____ – twenty-three
6 thirty-three – _____ – thirty-five
7 forty-six – _____ – forty-four
8 sixty – _____ – fifty-eight

C1
Was steht in der Wortschlange? Für welche Mahlzeiten würdest du die Sachen verwenden? Finde die Wörter und schreibe sie zur richtigen Mahlzeit. Manche Lebensmittel kannst du mehrfach zuordnen.

applesteamilkcornflakeschickenbaconcheeseeggssausagesbuttermarmaladeicecreamtoastchipsvegetablesonionsorangejuicebreadsugar

BREAKFAST

LUNCH

DINNER

Nun vergleicht eure Ergebnisse:

What's for breakfast?

Well, for breakfast there is / there are …

C2
So sieht es im Superstore in Hendon aus. Male die Dinge im Regal bunt aus.

Dann kannst du ein Ratespiel spielen: Du suchst dir einen Gegenstand auf deinem Regal aus, nennst ihn aber nicht. Dein/e Partner/in muss herausfinden, was es ist. Er/sie fragt:

Js it blue/red/ …?   Yes, it is.
　　　　　　　　　　No, it isn't.

Js it on the left/right / at the top/bottom / in the middle?

Dann tauscht ihr die Rollen.

C3 a) Wann ist Essenszeit? Schreibe auf:

1. 1:30 ☀ It's one thirty in the afternoon. It's time for lunch.

2. 7:30 🌅 It's _____ in the morning.
   It's time for _____.

3. 6:30 🌙 _____ in the evening.
   _____.

b) Wann sind DEINE/EURE Essenszeiten?

I have   breakfast _____.
         lunch   at _____.
         dinner   _____.

C4

a) Kannst du diese Wörter mit der Sortiermaschine richtig verteilen?

legs head teeth apples foot man nose
cornflakes girl cupboard feet
woman sister bathroom
dogs schoolbags table
houses pictures
skirt

pencil   *oranges*

Einzahl   Mehrzahl

b) Bilde die Mehrzahlendungen dieser Wörter:

1 park – (2) <u>two parks</u>

1 raincoat – (12) _____

1 shirt – (21) _____

1 skirt – (44) _____

1 drink – (39) _____

c) Sprich die Mehrzahlwörter aus. Welchen Unterschied gibt es zwischen den beiden Gruppen?

1 apple – (23) <u>twenty-three apples</u>

1 table – (26) _____

1 number – (66) _____

1 hand – (2) _____

1 chicken – (5) _____

zzz

sss

C5
Achte genau auf die Endungen, die du hörst. Ist es [s] oder [z]?
Versuche nach dem zweiten Hören die Wörter zu schreiben.
Dann lies sie deinem Nachbarn / deiner Nachbarin vor.

[s]	[z]
_____	_____
_____	_____
_____	_____
_____	_____

C6
Charlie und Mrs Williams unterhalten sich an der Kasse.
Wie teuer sind die einzelnen Artikel, die Charlie gekauft hat?
Überprüfe für Mrs Williams, ob die Kasse den Gesamtpreis richtig ausgedruckt hat.

ARTICLES	PRICE
yoghurt	_____
milk	_____
onions	_____
chips	_____
apples	_____
chicken	_____
cheese	_____
bread	_____
cornflakes	_____
sugar	_____
orange juice	_____
chocolate	_____
magazine	_____
TOTAL	£13.53
PAID	£15.00
CHANGE	£ 1.47

Detective page

D1 Jedes der folgenden Bilder steht für eine Tätigkeit, die du schon kennst.
Wie heißen die Verben auf Englisch?

_____listen_____   _____

_____   _____

_____   _____

_____

D2 Wie lange brauchst du, um diese Wörter nach dem Alphabet zu ordnen?

cornflakes – yoghurt – bacon – mother – pupil – kitchen – nose – drink – monster – hair – duck – dinner – head – egg – queue – price – hand – nice – leg

_____
_____
_____
_____
_____
_____
_____
_____

D3 Nicht alle Wörter, die sich reimen, werden auch ähnlich geschrieben.
Finde hier 10 Paare von Reimwörtern:

bike   write   book   late   eye   look   see   more ✓
door ✓   blue   hair   red   chair   like   eight
I   right   two   head   tea

door – more   _____ – _____
_____ – _____   _____ – _____
_____ – _____   _____ – _____
_____ – _____   _____ – _____
_____ – _____   _____ – _____

Detective page

D4 Finde Gegensätze zu mindestens 6 der folgenden Wörter:

1 slim _____
2 girl _____
3 Mr _____
4 brother _____
5 blonde _____
6 dark _____
7 tall _____
8 man _____
9 curly _____
10 food _____
11 warm _____
12 in front of _____

D5 Suche dir aus Theme 2 eine Person heraus, die du gerne magst. Schreibe so viel wie möglich über diese Person auf. Falls du Hilfe benötigst, schau ins Textbook S. 34 C4.

_____
_____
_____
_____
_____
_____
_____
_____
_____
_____
_____
_____
_____
_____

A1 Erinnerst du dich?

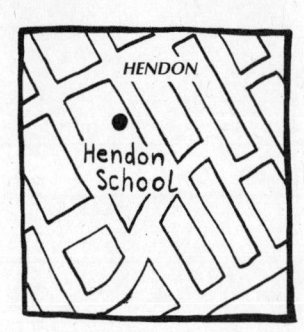

Holland Park School is in _____

Holland Park School is _____ school.

Hendon School is _____ school.

_____ is from _____ School.

_____ is from _____ School.

A2 In diesem Poster sind 9 Fehler versteckt. Finde und korrigiere sie.

It's Holland Park School Cup Final, not _____

_____
_____
_____
_____
_____
_____
_____
_____
_____

Hendon School Cup Final
HOLLAND PARK SCHOOL
against
HENDON SCHOOL

Sunday 10.00
Where: Holland Park
Yes, we sing in the final!
Come and watch our teachers!
Bring your schoolbooks!
Family and dogs welcome.

3

A3 Lies A3 im Textbook auf Seite 41.
Bilde Sätze aus diesen Wörtern:

1 team – have – girls – I – eleven – now – my – for
_____

2 about – your – what – team?
_____

3 come – Mary – can't
_____

4 pity – a – what – !
_____

5 ask – can – Susan – you – ?
_____

6 fast – she – run – can
_____

7 till – can't – Saturday – wait – I
_____

A4 Erinnerst du dich an Gillians und Veras Telefongespräch?

1. Vera erzählt Gillian, dass 11 Mädchen in ihrem Team sind.

2. Gillian erzählt Vera, dass Mary nicht kommen kann.

3. Vera bedauert das. Sie schlägt vor, Susan zu fragen.

> Oh dear! Can you ask Susan? I have 11 girls for my team now. Mary can't come.

A5 Schreibe auf, was diese Leute haben.

Brenda has _____

Charlie and his sister have _____

Vera _____

_____

_____

_____

_____

I _____

My friend _____

My teachers _____

My mother and my father _____

B1 Vervollständige die Sätze mit is/isn't, can/can't.

1 The Cup Final _____ on Saturday.

2 It _____ at Holland Park School.

3 Karim _____ find his school scarf.

4 Susan _____ run very fast.

5 Susan _____ in the goal.

6 Mary _____ come.

7 The girls' match _____ at 9.30.

What about football for girls? What do you think?

I think football for girls _____ interesting.

Girls _____ play football.

B2 Was können sie (+) und was nicht (–)? Schreibe 10 Sätze.

	run fast	kick a ball	speak English	stand on my/his/her head	count backwards	sing	play badminton	...	...	...
I										
My friend										
My father										
My mother										
My brother										
My sister										
My teacher										
My dog					–					
...										
...										
...										

Example: My dog can't sing.

B3 Wer kann was?

a) Sieh dir die Bilder an. Was meinst du?

1 Can this elephant play football?
   No, it can't. / J think it can. 
2 Can this monster play handball?
_____

3 What about this monster?
_____

4 Can this bike go fast?
_____

5 What about this bike?
_____

6 Can this boy sing?
_____

7 What about this boy?
_____

8 Can this girl skate?
_____

9 What about Susan?
_____

10 Can Gillian and Vera play table tennis?

11 What about Susan?
_____

Yes,	she / he / it	can.
No,	she / he / it / they	can't.

b) Bilde weitere Sätze.

_____
_____
_____

3

B4 Welche Sportarten sind hier gesucht?
Beschreibe DEINE drei Lieblingssportarten.

football   handball   tennis   riding   swimming   karate
basketball   streetball   table tennis   inline skating

My favourite sport is _____.

It is for boys and girls.

There are seven people in the team.

We can play it on a playing field or at a sports centre.

We can wear shorts and T-shirts and _____ boots.

My favourite sport is _____

It is for boys and girls.

You can do it alone or with friends.

You sit on a big animal.

You can wear jeans and boots.

B5 A sports puzzle

Where can you do a lot of sports? At the _____ (13)

B 6

a) Schreibe diese Wörter richtig sortiert in die drei Spalten.

hand, T-shirt, leg, team, boot, goal, player, head, ear, shoe, pullover, match, scarf, winner, nose, eye, foot, sweatshirt, kick

FOOTBALL	CLASSROOM	BODY

b) Jetzt finde die Mehrzahlformen von mindestens acht dieser Wörter.

B 7

In der Schülerzeitung sind die beiden Fußballberichte durcheinander geraten. Unterstreiche in zwei verschiedenen Farben, was zu welchem Bericht gehört. Schreibe die vollständigen Berichte auf. Dein Textbook (B5 S. 46) hilft dir dabei.

FANTASTIC MATCH IN THE CUP FINAL
Hendon girls beat Hendon School boys' team 2:1 in last minute.
Goals: Gillian Collins (2) and Brenda Tan Fong (1). Better luck next year, girls!

C1 Kreuze die richtigen Satzhälften an:

1. Susan, Karim and Gillian find a hedgehog …
   a. in the kitchen. ☐   b. on the road. ☐   c. in a park. ☐

2. They take the hedgehog …
   a. to Susan's flat. ☐   b. to the police station. ☐   c. to school. ☐

3. Susan's mother says they can give the hedgehog …
   a. some milk. ☐   b. some water. ☐   c. some snails. ☐

4. Susan's mother says it is …
   a. a wild animal. ☐   b. a lovely animal. ☐   c. a big animal. ☐

5. She says they must take the hedgehog …
   a. to the police station. ☐   b. back to the park. ☐   c. to the dog. ☐

6. Henrietta is the name of …
   a. Susan's sister. ☐   b. Susan's mother. ☐   c. the hedgehog. ☐

C2 Was erfährst Du über Henrietta? Schreibe Stichworte auf.

_____   _____

_____   _____

_____   _____

_____   _____

Benutze deine Notizen, um über Henrietta zu berichten.

C3 Höre dir dies Gespräch an und fülle die Lücken mit den Wörtern aus der Box.

The hungry _____

Susan: Look! I can see an animal! Can you _____ it, too, Karim?

Karim: Yes, and here I _____ it. Look!

Susan: Oh, it's _____.

Karim: Yes, it's nice. Hi there, Henry – or is it Henrietta?

Susan: Is it _____? What can we _____ it to _____?

Karim: Oh, _____, or perhaps some _____. Are there _____ at your house?

Susan: No, of course not. But _____ we can _____ snails here in the _____.

eat	have	lovely	perhaps	tea
find	hedgehog	milk	see	
give	hungry	park	snails	

C4 Wem gehört welches Tier?

Charlie Miss Tate Gillian Mr Carlucci David Brenda

Oscar Tick, Trick, Truck Esmeralda Toby Fuzzy Kenny

1. David has a dog. His name _____.
2. _____
3. _____
4. _____
5. _____
6. _____

C5 Pets in your class

a) Mach eine Umfrage in deiner Klasse, wer welches Haustier hat.

dog	Julia
cat	
hamster	Arne
hedgehog	
elephant	
...	
...	
...	
...	

b) Dann schreibe einen kurzen Bericht.

Julia, Murat and Ingo have dogs, but Petra has a cat. I have a guinea pig. Mr Wolter has no pet. No one has an elephant.

3

C 6 Was können diese Tiere (nicht) essen?

... can / can't eat ...

... is / isn't / are / aren't good for ...

Example: *Sausages aren't good for hamsters.*

C 7 Animal puzzle
Hier sind vier Tiere versteckt. Male sie an.

Beschreibe sie:

My animal no. 1 is a _____ (colour) _____ (animal).

_____

_____

_____

Detective page

D1 Wie viele Wörter mit diesen Buchstaben findest du in Theme 3?

nn: _____

ll: _____

tt: _____

mm: _____

k: _____

D2 Wie viele Sportarten kennst du, …

… für die man einen Ball braucht? _____

… die man nur drinnen betreibt? _____

D3 Wie viele Wörter kannst du bilden aus den Buchstaben von
BASKETBALL COACH?

_____

_____

_____

D4 Schau dir diese Wortliste aus Theme 3 an. Unterstreiche alle 18 Verben und schreibe sie auf. Wie heißen sie auf Deutsch?

about, against, all, animal, ask, bed, bird, box, bring, carrot, cat, come, difficult, do, eat, exciting, family, farm, fast, find, give, go, happy, house, last, lovely, match, near, next, nice, pet, pig, ride, run, shoe, sing, speak, stand, stop, story, take, then, very, wait, watch, wear, when, year

_____   _____

_____   _____

_____   _____

_____   _____

_____   _____

_____   _____

_____   _____

_____   _____

_____   _____

D5 Sieh dir die Liste in D4 noch einmal an und unterstreiche nun alle 9 Adjektive in einer anderen Farbe. Schreibe sie mit ihrer deutschen Bedeutung auf.

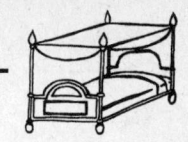

A1 Look at the picture of Vera's room in your textbook on page 52. Where are these things?

Example: **The inline skates are under the chair.**

The rucksack		on	the chair.
The elephants		over	the room.
The books		in	the desk.
The poster		under	the shelf/shelves.
The shelves	is	next to	the cupboard.
The CD player	are	in front of	the elephants.
The gorilla		behind	the rucksack.
The lamp		in the middle of	Vera's bed.
The comics			
The inline skates			
The extra bed			

A2 What can you say about Vera and Gillian on the phone? Look at page 52 in your textbook.

The extra bed in Vera's room is for _____

Vera likes _____

She has a lot of shelves for _____

She has a cupboard for _____

Gillian can bring _____

Vera's dad _____

Vera must make _____

A3 Where are these things in YOUR room?

I put my	books diary socks T-shirts shoes postcards inline skates …	on in under next to	the shelf/shelves. my bed. my desk. my cupboard. the wardrobe. …

A4 **A new room**
Listen to Charlie's friend.
Put the wardrobe, bed, cupboard and shelves in his room.

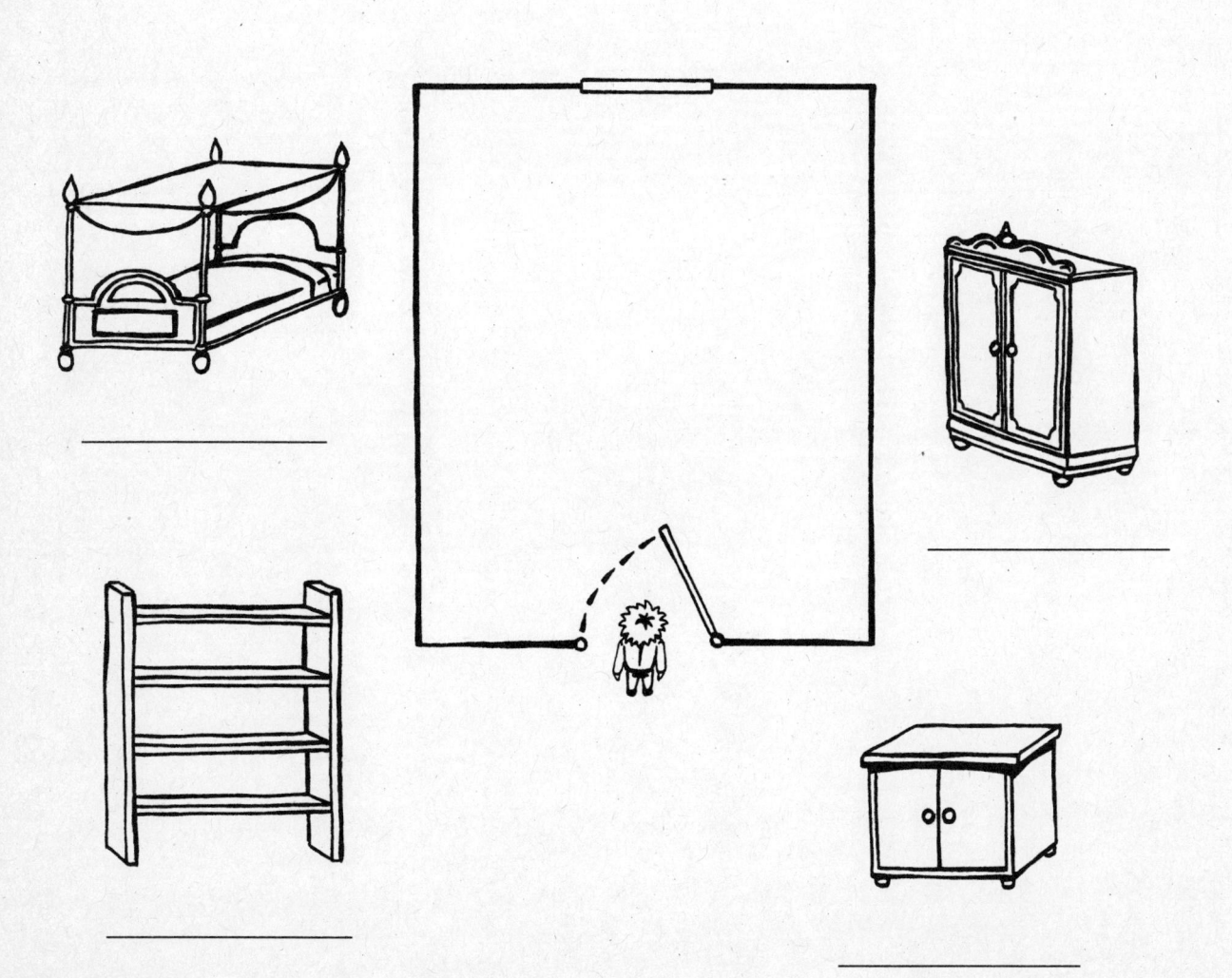

A5 YOUR dream room
Draw a plan of your dream room. Find pictures for your plan. Show the plan to your class.

You can write a text about your dream room. Here are some ideas for you:

My dream room
My dream room has a basketball basket so that I can play basketball every day. It is a big room.
On the wall there are grey elephants – my favourite animals. There is also a shelf for my elephants. My bed is in the middle of the room. I have a wardrobe and a cupboard. And, of course, a desk.

B1
What do you know about Vera and her family? Put crosses and then write sentences. You can look in your textbook.

	Vera	Vera's mum	Vera's dad
has an extra bed			
makes the salad			
cleans her room			
often does the cooking			
has nice posters			
has a small room			
puts flowers on the table			
likes elephants			

_____
_____
_____
_____
_____
_____
_____

B2
Write numbers for the correct order. You can look in your textbook on page 57.

- [ ] David works in the Superstore.
- [1] Gillian gets off the train.
- [ ] Vera has a lot of ideas for the weekend.
- [ ] Mr Coggins sells hot chestnuts.
- [ ] Vera meets Gillian at the exit.
- [ ] Kenny, David's dog, doesn't like the snow.
- [ ] Gillian and Vera buy two bags of hot chestnuts.
- [ ] Vera's father always makes spaghetti on Fridays.

B 3 What is the weather like? Can you find out?

1 We can _____ to my new CD.

2 Vera's dad makes _____ on Fridays.

3 Vera has a _____ in her room.

4 David helps his father in the shop _____ day.

5 Kenny _____ like the snow.

6 Gillian gets off the _____ at Hendon.

7 There is snow _____ .

8 Joe Coggins sells hot _____ .

9 It is late Friday _____ .

10 Vera has a lot of _____ .

11 Gillian comes to Vera on _____ .

And the weather? __ __'__ __ __ __ __ __ __ __ __ __.

B 4

a) What can the snowmen see in the park in summer and in winter?
Read the sentences and write "W" for winter and "S" for summer in the boxes.

- [S] 1 Boys and girls swim in the lake.
- [ ] 2 It is dark at five o'clock.
- [ ] 3 Everyone is cold.
- [ ] 4 The trees are green.
- [ ] 5 Birds sing.
- [ ] 6 Children go ice-skating on the lake.
- [ ] 7 There are a lot of flowers.
- [ ] 8 You can buy hot chestnuts.
- [ ] 9 People drink hot chocolate.
- [ ] 10 Everyone eats ice-cream.
- [ ] 11 The days are very long.
- [ ] 12 There is a snowman in the park.
- [ ] 13 People wear a lot of clothes.
- [ ] 14 Everyone wears T-shirts and shorts.

b) Can YOU write more sentences about summer and winter and draw a picture?

_____
_____
_____
_____

B5 a) When do YOU do these things?
Make lists.

watch TV   ride my bike   go inline skating   read comics   go ice-skating
go to the cinema   play badminton   listen to music   go swimming
play streetball   play football   stand on my head   play cards   go skiing

summer	winter	never

b) Now talk to your partner.

I always play football in summer. What about you?

I play football in summer and in winter.

I listen to music in summer and sometimes in winter. And you?

I always listen to music ....

I never play badminton in winter. And you?

...

C1 Can you find the correct order for the dialogue? Give the balloons a number and then act it. Look at page 59 in your textbook.

1 Come and meet my mum. Mum, this is Ron.

Nice to meet you.

Ron, what about some tea?

Oh, yes, lovely. Thank you.

Hello, Ron.

Hello, Mrs Fiorucci.

Nice to meet you, too.

C2 Put the words in the lists and speak about them. You can add more words, too.

hockey, handball, cornflakes, water, a cat/cats, coffee, sausages, milk, spaghetti, school, eggs, boys, football, fish, bacon, blue eyes, English, the weekend, snails, postcards, basketball, girls, tennis, ducks, a dog/dogs, ice-cream, skirts, table tennis, chocolate, Mondays, badminton, apples

I play	I don't play	I eat	I don't eat	I like	I don't like	I have	I don't have

C3 Who does what in your family?

cleans the windows? · does the cooking? · does the shopping? · cleans the vegetables?
takes out the rubbish? — **WHO** — cleans the bathroom?
cleans the kitchen? · tidies your room? · feeds the pets? · waters the flowers?

Examples: I feed the pets. I don't do the cooking.
My brother cleans the windows. My mum doesn't take out the rubbish.

_____
_____
_____
_____
_____
_____

C4 Read about Charlie's week in your textbook on page 61. Match these sentence parts and write them down.

On Sundays Charlie _____

Then Charlie goes back to bed and his mum _____

On Mondays Charlie and his sister Sharon _____

On Tuesdays Charlie _____

After training Charlie and his friends _____

On Wednesdays Charlie _____

On Thursdays Charlie _____

On Fridays Charlie's parents _____

Charlie babysits Sharon and they _____

On Saturdays Charlie and his dad sometimes _____

… go to ballet school.	… have baked beans.
… doesn't like school because he has art.	… makes breakfast.
… writes about goldfish.	… go to see an Arsenal match.
… makes his mum a cup of tea.	… goes to football training.
… go out.	… drink lemonade and talk.

C5 Write down the forms for the present tense first. Then find them in the puzzle.

```
W A T C H E S P T
A F S L I K E L H
T E Y E T A K E S
E E A A S N A H E
R D L N I T M I T
S S P R S N I A I
T I D I E S L A R
S E O G K K S A W
```

1. I play – he _____
2. we watch – she _____
3. we clean – you _____
4. you go – she _____
5. I feed – Charlie _____
6. they tidy – Gillian _____
7. you take – Sharon _____
8. we eat – it _____
9. I wait – it _____
10. they help – I _____
11. he does – they _____
12. he writes – she _____
13. I make – he _____
14. they like – I _____
15. we water – Vera _____
16. we drink – my parents _____
17. he talks – my friends _____
18. she asks – you _____

There are 5 extra letters. You do this all the time.

_ _ _ _ _

C6 Fill in one of these words: me – you – her – him – us – them

Example: Look, there are Vera and Gillian. Can't you ask ___them___?

1 "Here are some chocolates for _____, Vera."
2 "Can you come to the cinema with _____?"
3 Gillian takes the tube to Hendon. Vera meets _____ at the station.
4 On the way home she tells _____ the plans for the weekend.
5 The snowmen want to see the summer. The man with the freezer helps _____.
6 Vera introduces Gillian to her parents. Gillian can call _____ Janet and Dan.
7 David has a lot of work. Let's help _____.
8 "We need a new girl for our football team. Can you play for _____?"
9 "Please, can you give _____ your calculator?"
10 Vera's father does the cooking on Fridays. Vera helps _____.
11 "Nice to meet _____, Mr Gulbenkian."
12 "We want to go to the park tomorrow. Can you come with _____?"

Detective page

D1 Look at the word lists for themes 1–4 and find words with these letters:

sh: shop, _____

x: six, _____

y…: yes, _____

ee: three, _____

…y: boy, _____

D2 In theme 3 D4 you started to write a list of verbs. Look at theme 4 and add all the new verbs.

D3 Can you finish this?

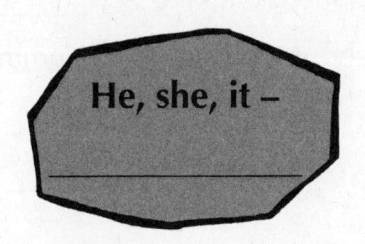

> He, she, it –
> _____

D4 Write down all the new information about your favourite person from theme 2.

_____
_____
_____
_____
_____
_____
_____
_____
_____

D5 Odd man out. There is always one wrong word. Find it, please.

a) spaghetti – bacon – milk – bread – chicken
b) onions – apples – carrots – chocolate – potatoes
c) morning – afternoon – summer – evening – night
d) gorilla – elephant – goldfish – hedgehog – guinea-pig
e) tube – desk – chair – wardrobe – cupboard
f) hot – snow – ice-cream – flowers – green

Perhaps you can make your own puzzles.

Detective page

D 6 Find all the adjectives in themes 3 and 4: great, friendly, hot, …

_____

_____

_____

_____

D 7 Use a stopwatch!
How fast can you find all the answers?

1. The gorilla is on page _____.
2. Who puts flowers on the table on page 55? _____.
3. What is the snowman's nose in the photo on page 57? _____.
4. What is the first word of the story about the snowmen's summer holiday?

   _____.
5. Why doesn't Charlie like Thursdays? _____

   _____.
6. Who says "I always clean my bike." on page 60? _____.
7. Write down five things you can see in the pictures on page 58.

   _____.
8. What is not in Vera's room?

   TV – elephants – chair – comics – books – gorilla – flowers – wardrobe.
9. How many pencils are there on page 53? _____.
10. Who has a box of onions on page 57? _____.
11. What is the colour of Gillian's jacket on page 60? _____.
12. Gillian gets on the tube at _____.

A1

**a) What can you see from a balloon?
Draw a picture and write the words.**

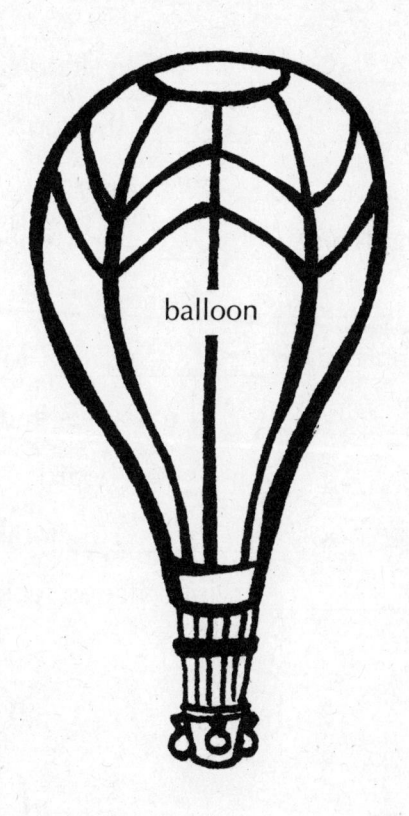

balloon

b) Write a text:

From my balloon I can see _____

_____

There is / There are _____

_____

In my balloon I can fly to _____

_____

A2 What can you say about Charlie's classmates?

Use these verbs: watch play like have go water do clean

VERB

like	1 Serafin ___likes___ inline skating.
_____	2 All the girls _____ the sports teacher.
_____	3 Tim _____ table tennis.
_____	4 Sandy and Jenny _____ dogs.
_____	5 Pedro _____ karate.
_____	6 William and Sarah _____ to ballet school.
_____	7 Clare _____ the flowers in the classroom.
_____	8 Nobody _____ the board.
_____	9 A lot of the boys _____ football at the weekend.
_____	10 Judy _____ information technology.

He, she, it – -s must fit.

A3 Write a quiz about YOUR classmates.
a) Work with a partner and write down six sentences or more.
b) Do not say the names and let other classmates guess.

Examples:
They don't like "Bayern München". Who are they?
He likes biology and plays hockey. Who is it?

A4

a) Write down YOUR timetable.

Lesson Time	1	2	3	4	5	6
Monday						
Tuesday						
Wednesday						
Thursday						
Friday						

b) What is your number one subject, number two and so on?
Make a list. Start with your favourite subject.

1 _____
2 _____
3 _____
4 _____
5 _____
… _____

c) Work in small groups. Talk and write about your lists.

My favourite subject is _____ and I like _____, too.

_____ is sometimes interesting and sometimes boring.

I don't like _____. _____ is difficult for me.

A5

a) Look at Charlie's timetable on page 68 in your textbook and at your timetable.
Fill in the list of all the subjects. Now put crosses:

What subjects are on Charlie's timetable?   What subjects are on your timetable?

Charlie	Subjects	My subjects
☐	_____	☐
☐	_____	☐
☐	_____	☐
☐	_____	☐
☐	_____	☐
☐	_____	☐
☐	_____	☐
☐	_____	☐
☐	_____	☐
☐	_____	☐
☐	_____	☐
☐	_____	☐

b) Now talk about the subjects with a partner.

Charlie has … but we have …

Charlie has … – Yes, and we have …, too.

Charlie doesn't have … – We don't have …

A6

Listen to this story of Mr Graham's adventure in Florida.
Put the pictures into the correct order.
Then listen to the story again and colour the pictures.

A7

a) Find all the questions in the Morning song in your textbook on page 69. Write them down.

_____
_____
_____
_____
_____
_____
_____
_____
_____
_____
_____
_____
_____
_____

b) Answer six questions.

c) Then work with a partner and answer four more questions.

d) Go to the board with your partner and write down the difficult questions. You can answer them in class, with your teacher.

B1 Fill in the right words.

The (ninth/nine) _____ month is September.

June is the (sixth/six) _____ month.

The (fifth/five) _____ month is May.

Every four years, February has (twenty-nine/twenty-ninth) _____ days.

The last day of November is the (thirtieth/thirty) _____.

The 31st December is the (last/first) _____ day of the year.

December is the (twelfth/twelve) _____ month.

August is the (eighth/eight) _____ month.

The first day of the year is the (first/one) _____ of January.

October has (thirty-first/thirty-one) _____ days.

B2 When are their birthdays? Write the dates down.

My birthday is on the twenty-first day of the year.
21st January

My birthday is on the second day of the fifth month.
_____

My birthday is on the last day of the eighth month.
_____

My birthday is on the fifteenth day of the eleventh month.
_____

My birthday is on the fifty-third day of the year.
_____

My birthday is on the thirty-first day of the last month.
_____

My birthday is on the fourth day of the sixth month.
_____

My birthday is on the nineteenth day of the tenth month.
_____

B3 Karim goes to the market and he can see a lot of people. Find out who does what. You can look at your textbook on pages 72/73.

Use these verbs: buy go have like see sell

He, she, it – -s must fit.

Karim _____ to the market.
Mr Ram _____ fruit and vegetables.
Mr Tan _____ clothes.
Mrs Gale _____ a music stall with hundreds of records.
Karim _____ a good poster.
Mrs Fiorucci _____ broccoli.
The man at Mr Tan's stall _____ the red and white T-shirt.
Karim _____ the balloon poster for £2.50.

B4 a) Find questions to these answers. You can look at your textbook on pages 72/73.

1 _____? Yes, I like this black cap.
2 _____? It's £4.75.
3 _____? Sorry, I don't have bananas today.
4 _____? That's a fantastic idea.
5 _____? Yes, please.

Can I have some bananas, please?   Can I help you?   What about a poster for David's room?   How much is this CD?   Do you want this poster?

b) Can you find more questions?

1 _____? It's on 5th July.
2 _____? Biology.
3 _____? 6.
4 _____? No, thank you.
5 _____? At 7 o'clock.

_____
_____
_____

B 5 It's your friend's birthday tomorrow. What can you buy?

a) What does your friend like?

☐ books
☐ computer games
☐ sports
☐ music
☐ games
☐ art
☐ …

b) Look at the catalogue page. What can you buy for your friend?

My/our friend likes _____
_____
_____
_____
_____

I/we can buy a/some _____ or I/we can buy a/some _____ .

c) Look at the catalogue page again.

What can you buy for under £ 2, under £ 5, under £ 8?
What can you buy for over £ 8?

Example: *You can buy a model car for £ 1.99.*

_____
_____
_____
_____
_____
_____
_____
_____
_____

Monster heroes from
£ 3.89

£ 20.- each

£ 30.-

Model cars from
£ 1.99

Teddies
£ 7.25

Baseball caps
3 colours
£ 3.90

T-Shirts
5 colours
£ 7.90

Books from
£ 3.-

Sports watch
£ 10.30

Rollerskates
£ 19.95

Table tennis set
£ 11.99

Basketball
£ 8.50

Skateboard
£ 22.95

Inlineskaters
£ 26.95

B 6 Match the words in the three lists. Draw lines like this:

my	them	she
your	us	they
her	me	we
his	you	I
its	it	it
our	him	he
their	her	you

Now use some of the words in these sentences.

1 My name is Robin. _____ 'm from Nottingham. _____ favourite sport is cricket. You can watch _____ in the school team.

2 Karim sees a lovely poster. _____ buys _____ for David's birthday.

3 Mrs Fiorucci is back in London. _____ buys vegetables for _____ dinner.

4 "Karim, can _____ come to _____ party on Saturday? _____ can play games and listen to CDs. My mum has ice-cream and lemonade for _____."

5 Mrs Gale has hundreds of records. _____ are not new, so she sells _____ half-price.

6 Mr Graham can't find _____ maths book today. So _____ tells one of _____ balloon stories. All the pupils listen to _____.

B 7 Here are some scrambled questions about Karim at the market. Write the questions and short answers.

1 go – does – birthday party – Karim – when – to David's?

When does Karim go to David's birthday party?
_____

_____

2 Karim – does – go – where?

_____

_____

3 does – what – sell – Mr Ram?

_____

_____

4 see – what – Karim – does – at Mr Tan's stall?

_____

_____

5 how much – cost – does – the poster?

_____

_____

B 8 a) How many questions can you ask?

drink play sleep clean write read
WHEN DO YOU ...?   WHERE DO YOU ...?   WHAT DO YOU ...?
make go buy watch meet
eat

What do you read in bed?

b) Interview your partner. Ask him/her six questions and answer his/her questions.

C1
Read page 75 in your textbook again, look at the pictures and listen to the CD.
Fill in the list:

David's family:	David's friends:	David's presents:

C2
a) It is almost 4 o'clock on David's birthday. Who is doing what?

1 David is waiting _____.

2 David's mother _____.

3 David's father _____.

4 His grandmother and grandfather _____.

5 His Aunt Fay and his Uncle Morgan _____.

6 They are all _____.

7 Kenny _____.

b) Now it is 7 o'clock. What are they doing now?
You can use these verbs:

read – play – sleep – talk – drink – eat   + -ing!

1 Uncle Morgan is dancing.

2 _____

3 _____

4 _____

5 _____

6 _____

7 _____

8 _____

C3 There are two stories mixed up here. Can you write the two stories down? Underline the sentences first, perhaps blue for story 1 and red for story 2 or _____ (Story 1) and _____ (Story 2).

Find good titles for the stories, too.

James has an invitation to Sally's birthday party.
Mr Steel is Nick's history teacher.
The party is on Friday evening.
But James doesn't have a birthday present.
He's not a very good teacher, but he's a great jazz singer.
So he goes to the market in Portobello Road.
He sometimes tells his class about his concerts.
Nick listens to him and often thinks up his own music.
He stops at Mrs Kelly's stall.
Then he plays in concert with his teacher.
But there are only things for children.
He goes to the next stall and sees a poster of Sally's favourite pop group.
Everyone sings and dances.
It costs £4.25.
James buys it.
But then he wakes up.
A poster is a great present for Sally.
The history lesson is over.

C4 a) **Work with a partner and ask her/him about his birthday. Write her/his answers down.**

When is your birthday? _____.

Who comes to your party? _____
_____.

What do you do? _____
_____
_____
_____
_____

What do you eat? _____
_____
_____
_____

Where do you go? _____
_____
_____
_____

b) **Now write about your partner's birthday and then about YOUR birthday.**

_____'s birthday is in _____

Her/his guests are _____
_____

They _____
_____
_____
_____

My birthday _____

My _____
_____

We _____
_____
_____

C5 After the party David finds a lot of things. Whose things are they? Do you know? Ask your partner.

Whose raincoat is this?   _I think it's Uncle Morgan's._

Whose glasses are these?   _I think they are ..._

_____

_____

_____

_____

_____

_____

C6 Fill in the names of the people.

1 Folk music is ____Uncle Morgan's____ favourite music.
2 _____ cauliflowers are always fresh.
3 Mr Graham is _____ maths teacher.
4 The children and the teachers watch _____ balloon.
5 At _____ clothes stall you can buy T-shirts in all colours.
6 The poster looks good in _____ room.
7 _____ holiday is over.
8 David is _____ cousin.
9 The poster is _____ present for David.

Karim   David   Mr Graham   Mr Ram

Mrs Fiorucci   Charlie   Mr Tan   Gillian

C7 Find out what is right. You can look at C5 on page 78 in your textbook.

Example:
Thomas is Alice's ☒ husband ☐ mother ☐ sister (3)
husband (3) = (3rd letter) = S

1 David is Ivor's   ☐ son   ☐ uncle   ☐ grandson   (5)
2 Ivor is Janet's   ☐ father   ☐ aunt   ☐ husband   (5)
3 Thomas is Gillian's   ☐ uncle   ☐ father   ☐ cousin   (1)
4 Ivor is Gillian's   ☐ father   ☐ grandfather ☐ uncle   (1)
5 Thomas is Morgan's   ☐ cousin   ☐ son   ☐ brother   (5)
6 Gwen is Thomas's   ☐ husband   ☐ uncle   ☐ sister   (4)
7 Gillian is Gwen's   ☐ sister   ☐ daughter   ☐ aunt   (7)
8 Janet is Morgan's   ☐ mother   ☐ grandmother ☐ sister   (6)

Solution: __ __ __ __ __ __ __ __
          1 2 3 4 5 6 7 8

C8 Find the words in the pictures!

1 (shirt, h=k) — skirt
2 (mouse, m=h) — _____
3 (tree, t=th) — _____
4 (cake, c=l) — _____
5 (l + egg, ✗) — _____
6 (pond, k=t) — _____
7 (chair, ✗) — _____
8 (balloon, ll=c, ✗) — _____

Detective page

D1 Find the plurals of these words from theme 5:

story – _____ Friday – _____

child – _____ tooth – _____

birthday – _____ party – _____

wish – _____ tomato – _____

family – _____ box – _____

D2 Look at your verb list in D4 on page 33 in this WB. Add all the new verbs you can find in theme 5.

D3 Look through theme 5 in your textbook and find:

– 5 weekdays
– 5 months
– 5 girls' names
– 5 boys' names
– 5 birthday presents
– 5 family members
– 5 school subjects

D4 Look at the pictures on pages 66/67 in your textbook.
Say what the people in the pictures are doing.

D5 Look at your list of adjectives in D5 on page 33 in this WB. Add all the new adjectives from theme 5.

D6 Use your dictionary and find out what these words are in German:

headteacher: _____ whose: _____

history: _____ vegetables: _____

art: _____ food: _____

boring: _____ noisy: _____

And what are these in English?

schwierig: _____ vielleicht: _____

Einladung: _____ tanzen: _____

Erdkunde: _____ vorstellen: _____

Leute: _____ Ehemann: _____

D7 My top ten words in theme 5:

6

A1 Write your own notices. What do you want to sell? For how much?
Look at pages 80/81 in your textbook for help.

> A super buy!
> For only £1 per packet!
> **TRICK CHEWING GUM**
> (makes your tongue black)
> **CHAN'S TRICK SHOP**
> **QUEENSWAY**

Find a good beginning! _____

YOUR article: _____

describe it: _____

price: _____

YOUR name & phone number: _____

You can also draw your article!
Write your notices on cards and put them up in your classroom.

A2 Where do most of Roland's stamps come from?
Look at the map and fill in the words for the countries.

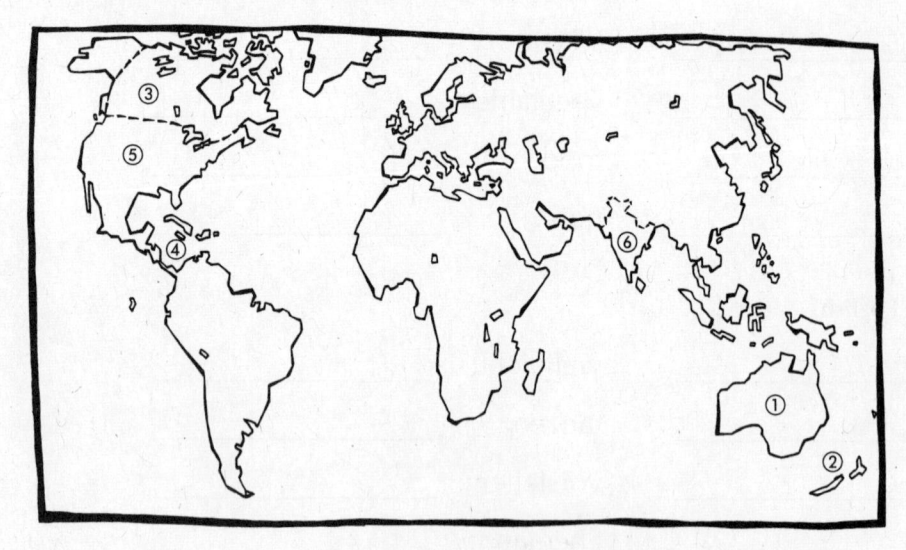

Solution:

6 = __ __ __ __ __

A3 a) Choose a club and fill in the form:

Holland Park School Football Club

Name: _____

Address: _____
_____

Class: _____

Do you have a) football boots? YES ☐ NO ☐
                    b) T-shirts and shorts? YES ☐ NO ☐
Do you have time on Saturday afternoons? YES ☐ NO ☐
Can you come to training on Wednesday evenings? YES ☐ NO ☐

Hendon Hackers Computer Club

Name: _____ Class: _____

Address: _____
_____

Do you have a computer? YES ☐   NO ☐
If yes, what sort is it? _____
What programs do you have? _____
_____
Do you have time on Tuesday evenings? YES ☐   NO ☐

HPPC HOLLAND PARK PET CLUB

Name: _____

Address: _____
_____

Class: _____

How many pets do you have? _____
What sort of pets do you have? _____
Do you want a pet? What sort? _____
Do you have time on Friday afternoons? YES ☐   NO ☐

b) YOUR club

Are you a member of a club? _____

What is the name of your club? _____

What do you do? _____

c) Make a list of clubs on the board. How many clubs are there in your class?

d) What about a new club? Do you have an idea?
Work with a partner. Make a poster and a membership form.

6

A4 Who has/likes/plays/collects what?

Example: Number 1 collects/likes cars. I think his name is Mr Fast.

A5 When can you do these sports and hobbies?
Put a cross when you can do what.

	January	February	March	April	May	June	July	August	September	October	November	December
collect stamps	+											
go swimming in a lake												
play tennis outside												
make a snowman												
listen to CDs												
read comics												
go skateboarding												
…												

Now write four or more sentences like this:

I can collect stamps in January but I can't go swimming in a lake.

I can collect stamps all year but I can't make a snowman all year.

_____
_____
_____
_____
_____
_____

A6 Listen to the CD/cassette (A5).
What are the children talking about? Write the sentences to the right clubs.

The film was a bit boring.
I looked at the photo exhibition first.
It was a bit like a ballet.
Brenda Tan Fong played solo trumpet.
I looked at a lot of stars and there was a very interesting talk about planets.
Then I looked through the microscope.
I learned how to make a camera.
Judy's song was "Way down south".
Well, first I watched a film.
I learned a lot of new names.
They danced backwards and forward.

School Band:
_____
_____

Nature Club:
_____
_____

Astronomy Club:
_____
_____

Photo Club:
_____
_____

Taekwon-do:
_____
_____

A7 a) Match the two verb forms: b) Put them in two groups:

play   learned
watch   missed
be   collected
look   danced
have   played
collect watched
learn   was/were
miss   looked
dance   had

easy	difficult

B1 Which animal/s? Look at pages 86/87 in your textbook.

It was eating the boy's rucksack. _____

Susan wanted to ride it. _____

It liked a boy's red T-shirt. _____

There was a song about them. _____

They had thirteen lambs. _____

They smelled terrible. _____

B2 What is funny in this picture?

bull   tractor   wearing   duck   riding   football
cleaning   lamb
goat   skirt
eating   T-shirt
chicken   pony
banana   glasses   dog   feet   playing

Example: The farmer is wearing a skirt.

The pig is _____

_____

_____

_____

_____

_____

6

B 3 Where are you?

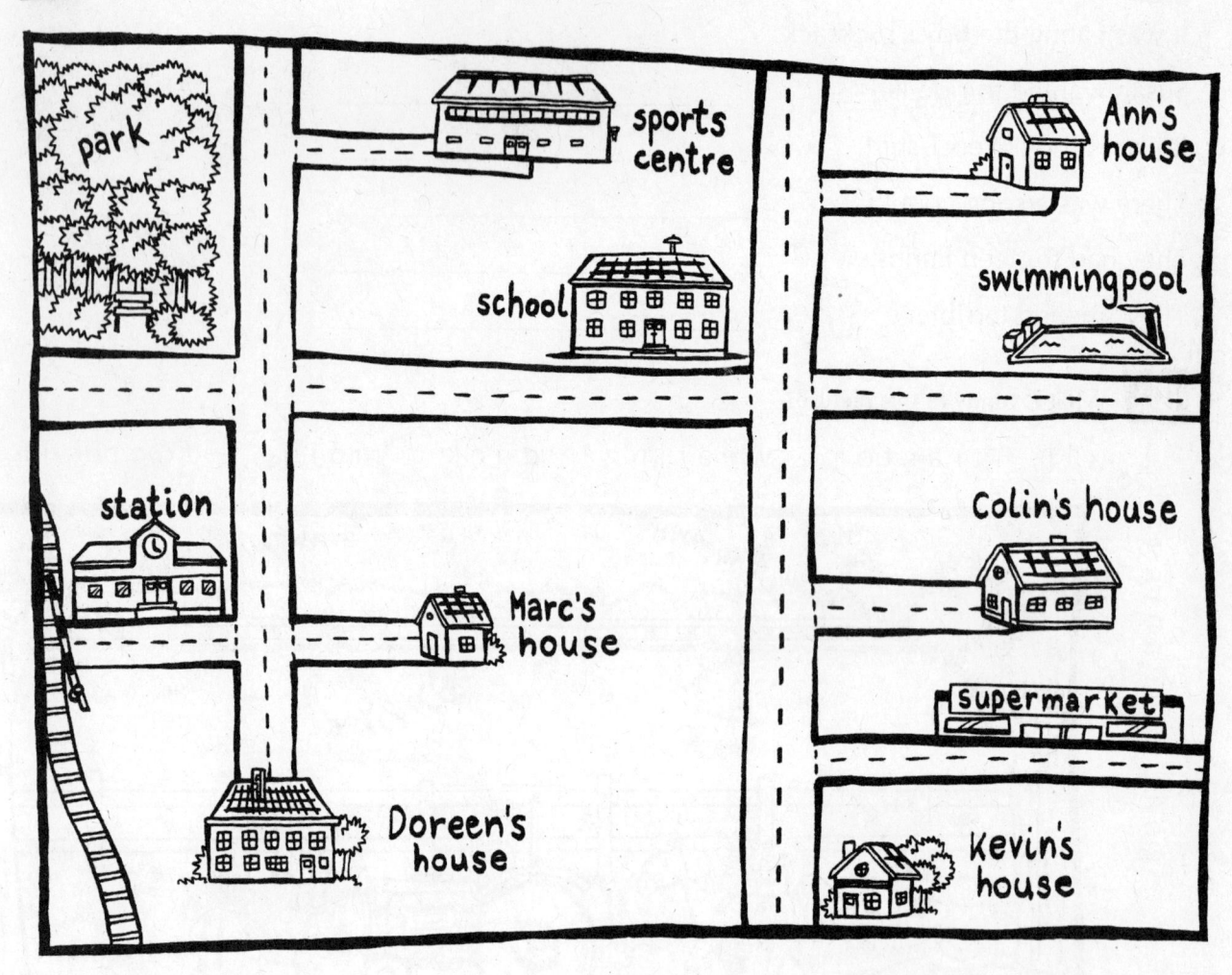

a) Look at the map and find out:

1. Start at Kevin's house. Go straight on. Take the third right. Where are you?

___

2. Start at Doreen's house. Turn left. Where are you?

___

turn left/right …

b) Now you write:

Start at ___

___

___

___

___

Then swap your workbook with a partner.

B 4 a) Find the plurals and write them in the lists.

pony sheep cat lamb Friday class library
baby horse city country child piglet
glass

LiF→no. 20

– ies –	– s –	– es –	!! (difficult)

b) Find more plurals. Look at your word lists.

B 5 Susan's afternoon at the farm was very exciting. Her dog had an interesting day, too. Can you tell the story?

walk to the park – look at ducks – play with a balloon – listen to a band – watch a hedgehog – visit some friends – have a chat with a lovely black poodle

"Well, Susan, at three o'clock I walked to the park and _____
_____
_____
_____
_____
_____
_____"

B6 Read "The storm at sea" in your textbook again.

a) What do you know?

The police are looking for a boat. ☐
The police have a boat. ☐
The police think Mr Goldman is a nice person. ☐
The police think there is something wrong with Mr Goldman. ☐

Mr Goldman was in a boat. ☐
Mr Goldman has size 9 boots. ☐
Mr Goldman was on a train. ☐
Mr Goldman has no boots. ☐

Jill's boot was in the water. ☐
Jill's boot was in the boat. ☐
Jill doesn't like sailing. ☐
Jill was the winner of a sailing competition. ☐

There were two people in the boat. ☐
There was only one person in the boat. ☐
There was a storm. ☐
It was dark. ☐

**b) What do you want to know? Write some questions down.
You can begin like this:**

Why was …? What was …? Was there …? Was …? Were …?

_____

_____

_____

B7 Now look for answers in part 2:

Scene: At the police station. Jill Goldman, Mr Goldman and Detective Blake sit at a desk.

Jill: OK. This is the story. We …

Mr Goldman: Don't tell him, Jill.

Jill: I must, Daddy. There was a bag in the water, near the beach. We opened it and it was full of gold coins. We wanted to sell them. Then there was the storm. We were in the water. And the bag with the gold coins – "Crash!" – and we …

Detective Blake: OK, Miss Goldman. Let's look for that bag of gold tomorrow.

C1 Read the RJE programme on page 90 in your textbook again.
You like music? What programme can you listen to? Go on.

	PROGRAMME	TIME
music		
hobbies		
sports		
nature		
news		
film		

C2

TV Programme

Tuesday		Wednesday		Thursday	
4.40	Pet Corner	4.35	English	4.40	Star Watch
5.10	_____	4.50	_____	5.00	_____
5.35	_____	5.40	Super Car	5.15	_____
6.00	_____	6.00	_____	6.00	_____

Can you fill in the TV programme? These sentences help you:

1 Animal Safari is on Wednesday before Super Car.

2 The Monster Game is on Thursday after Star Watch.

3 Big Cartoon is on Tuesday before the News.

4 Animal Quiz is on Thursday.

5 The News is at six o'clock every day.

6 Zappadak is on Tuesday after Pet Corner.

C3

	Yes, I do	No, I don't	Yes, I can	No, I can't	Yes, I am	No, I'm not
Are you a sports fan?	☐	☐	☐	☐	☐	☐
Do you like music from Scotland?	☐	☐	☐	☐	☐	☐
Do you watch football on TV?	☐	☐	☐	☐	☐	☐
Can you watch TV in the evening?	☐	☐	☐	☐	☐	☐
Can you speak French?	☐	☐	☐	☐	☐	☐
Do you get up at 7 o'clock on Sundays?	☐	☐	☐	☐	☐	☐
Are you a good hockey player?	☐	☐	☐	☐	☐	☐
Are you a pop fan?	☐	☐	☐	☐	☐	☐
Can you stand on your head?	☐	☐	☐	☐	☐	☐
Do you eat cornflakes for breakfast?	☐	☐	☐	☐	☐	☐
Can you make spaghetti?	☐	☐	☐	☐	☐	☐
Are you interested in computers?	☐	☐	☐	☐	☐	☐
Do you have friends outside Europe?	☐	☐	☐	☐	☐	☐
Can you draw a mouse?	☐	☐	☐	☐	☐	☐
Are you a member of a club?	☐	☐	☐	☐	☐	☐

a) Put YOUR crosses first. Then ask a partner and put his/her crosses in a different colour.

b) Write a text about your partner.

Example: Peter doesn't like music from Scotland. He watches football on TV.

___

c) Use YOUR answers for your cassette in textbook C5 on page 94.

C4 Here are words from theme 6. Are they nouns, verbs or adjectives?

old, swap, big, watch, buy, lovely, hear, size, white, make, sell, library, collect, favourite, pets, wash, bridge, exciting, new, camera, pond, wild, goat, interesting, ice-skates, listen, small, bite, news

Write them down in these lists:

NOUNS	VERBS	ADJECTIVES
size	collect	old

C5 The Junior breakfast show is on every morning from 7.30 to 9.00 o'clock. You can write to RJE and ask them to play a song for you or for a friend. Read Kevin's letter and then write your own.

Dear Tony,

I live in Bradford-on-Avon, near Bath, in England. A lot of people come here for their holidays in the summer. I always listen to your show in the morning before I go to school. My hobbies are cricket, swimming, model cars and, of course, listening to RJE. My favourite subject at school is information technology but I hate art. Please can you play "Moondance" by the Street Boys for my friend in Germany. Her name is Katrin Utsch and she lives in Frankfurt. It's her birthday on 26th June. Thanks a lot.

Best wishes

Kevin Pringle

PS. Please can you send me your autograph for my sister.

6 Detective page

D1 In theme 2 you started to write about your favourite person in this book. Add all the new information you can find.

D2 Add new words to your list of adjectives and to your list of verbs.

D3 And now: Take your stopwatch and GO!

a) Write down 5 countries outside Europe: _____
_____

b) How many notices are on the notice board on page 80/81 in the textbook?

c) What are these animals in English?

Ente _____   Ferkel _____   Schaf _____

Ziege _____   Lamm _____   Bulle _____

d) Was sagst du, wenn du wissen möchtest:

– wo die Toiletten sind: _____

– wo du etwas zu trinken kaufen kannst: _____

– ob es Postkarten zu kaufen gibt: _____

e) Look at pages 86/87 in your textbook. What are they doing?

The	ducks		sitting near the kiosk.
	bull		playing under the trees.
	pigs and piglets		looking at the girls.
	goat	is	looking at the dog.
	sheep and lambs	are	standing in front of the boy.
	dog		eating a rucksack.
	cat		eating grass.
	ponies		swimming on the water.

f) Who wants to sell ice-skates on page 80 in the textbook?

g) Can Karim go to the software library on Tuesday at 3.30pm?

D4 Your first year of English is over. Write down ...

- your favourite theme
- your favourite person in this book.
- your favourite page in the book.
- what you can say about YOU after this year.
- your top ten English words.

Die Verbformen

1 Formen von „be"

Langform	Kurzform	
I am	I'm	*ich bin*
you are	you're	*du bist / Sie sind*
he is	he's	*er ist*
she is	she's	*sie ist*
it is	it's	*es ist*
we are	we're	*wir sind*
you are	you're	*ihr seid / Sie sind*
they are	they're	*sie sind*

- Die Formen von **be** *(sein)* heißen *am, is* und *are*.
- Beim Sprechen benutzt man die **Kurzform,** beim Schreiben oft die **Langform.**
- Die Kurzform von *is* wird häufig auch nach anderen Wörtern benutzt: *what's, who's, there's, that's.*

2 Fragen und Kurzantworten

- Im Englischen antwortet man auf Fragen, die man mit *ja* oder *nein* beantworten kann, nicht nur *yes* oder *no*. Das klingt etwas unhöflich. Deshalb fügt man eine zusätzliche Bestätigung oder Ablehnung hinzu *(Yes, it is./No, it isn't.).*
- In bejahenden Antworten kann man die Kurzform (z. B. *you're*) nicht verwenden, in verneinenden Antworten schon.

Am I late?
No, you aren't.
Are you up?
Yes, I am.

Frage	bejahende Antwort	verneinende Antwort
Is Susan *(= she)* from Hendon?	Yes, she is.	No, she isn't.
Is Charlie *(= he)* from Hendon, too?	Yes, he is.	No, he isn't.
Is the butter *(= it)* on the table?	Yes, it is.	No, it isn't.
Are we all ready?	Yes, we are.	No, we aren't.
Are David and Susan *(= they)* here?	Yes, they are.	No, they aren't.
Are her jeans *(= they)* blue?	Yes, they are.	No, they aren't.

Die Verbformen

3 Das Verb „have"

- Mit dem Verb **have** kann man ausdrücken, was man hat.
- In der 3. Person Einzahl (bei *he, she, it* oder bei Namen, für die man *he, she, it* einsetzen kann) benutzt man **has**.

I	have	11 girls for our team.	ich habe
You	have	a nice school scarf.	du hast
He	has	blue eyes.	er hat
Gillian	has	a grey skirt.	sie hat
The car	has	four airbags.	es hat
We	have	a great idea.	wir haben
You	have	red T-shirts.	ihr habt
They	have	a match on Saturday.	sie haben

4 Das Hilfsverb „can/can't"

- Mit dem Hilfsverb **can** sagt man, was jemand tun kann, mit **can't**, was man nicht tun kann oder darf.
- **Can** und **can't** wird in allen Personen benutzt.

I **can** run fast.

No, you **can't** have a coke now but you **can** have an ice-cream.

Ich kann schnell laufen.

Du darfst jetzt keine Cola trinken, aber du darfst ein Eis essen.

- Auch Fragen und Antworten mit **can** und **can't** werden immer mit derselben Form gebildet.

Can she come?

Yes, she **can**.

Can we bring the hedgehog in the house?

No, you **can't**.

Die Verbformen

5 Die einfache Gegenwart (simple present)

I	play
you	play
he	play**s**
she	play**s**
it	play**s**
we	play
you	play
they	play

> He, she, it –
> -s must fit.

- Die einfache Gegenwartsform benutzt man, wenn man über Gewohnheiten oder regelmäßig vorkommende Ereignisse spricht. Man benutzt sie auch, wenn man beschreibt, dass jemand mehrere Dinge nacheinander tut (z. B. in einer Geschichte).
- Genau wie im Deutschen haben die Verben im Englischen nicht für alle Personen die gleichen Endungen. (man sagt *ich gehe,* aber *er geht* und *wir gehen*).
  Im Englischen braucht man sich nur zwei Formen zu merken:
- Das *simple present* hat dieselbe Form wie der Infinitiv, z. B. *play.* Nur in der 3. Person Einzahl (*he – she – it*) wird einfach ein **-s** angehängt.
- Endet das Verb mit einem Zischlaut oder einem **-s,** muss bei *he, she, it* ein **-es** angehängt werden:

You	wash	your face.
He	wash**es**	his face.

I	pass	the supermarket.
She	pass**es**	the supermarket.

- Achtung! Besondere Schreibweisen:

I	do	the cooking.
He	do**es**	the cooking.

We	go	to the football match.
She	go**es**	to the football match.

They	tidy	their room.
He	tid**ies**	his room.

> I play football.

6 Die Verneinung der einfachen Gegenwart

- Man verneint Sätze in der Gegenwart mit **don't**. Bei *he, she, it* benutzt man **doesn't**.
- Meistens benutzt man die Kurzformen. Die Langform von *don't* heißt *do not;* die von *doesn't* heißt *does not.*

I	**don't**	make my bed.	Ich mache mein Bett nicht.
You	**don't**	like ballet.	Du magst kein Ballett.
He	**doesn't**	like the snow.	Er mag keinen Schnee.
It	**doesn't**	eat potatoes.	Es isst keine Kartoffeln.
She	**doesn't**	say "Dad".	Sie sagt nicht „Dad".
We	**don't**	clean the board.	Wir putzen die Tafel nicht.
You	**don't**	water the flowers.	Ihr gießt die Blumen nicht.
They	**don't**	like the summer.	Sie mögen den Sommer nicht.

- Sätze, die Hilfsverben (z. B. *can*) enthalten, werden nicht mit *don't* verneint:
  I can't find my scarf.

Die Verbformen

7 Fragen in der einfachen Gegenwart: Entscheidungsfragen

- Es gibt im Englischen wie im Deutschen Entscheidungsfragen, die man mit „ja" oder „nein" beantwortet. Diese Fragen kann man mit einem Hilfsverb bilden, z. B.
  Can you come here?
- Entscheidungsfragen können auch mit *do/does* gebildet werden.

Frage			Kurzantwort	
Do	you know Mr Graham?		Yes, I do.	No, I don't.
Does	he tell nice stories?		Yes, he does.	No, he doesn't.
Does	Mrs Fiorucci buy broccoli?		Yes, she does.	No, she doesn't.
Does	a hedgehog like snails?		Yes, it does.	No, it doesn't.
Do	the children like Mr Graham's stories?		Yes, they do.	No, they don't.

8 Fragen in der einfachen Gegenwart: Bestimmungsfragen

- Um zu erfahren, wann, wo, was passiert oder passiert ist, stellt man Bestimmungsfragen. Diese Fragen bildet man mit Fragewörtern: **what**   was?
  when   wann?
  where   wo?
  why   warum?

What	**do**	you eat for breakfast?
Where	**does**	she eat breakfast?
Why	**does**	Mr Graham tell stories?
When	**do**	we have maths?

> Bei *he, she, it* musst du *does* verwenden.

9 Die Verlaufsform der Gegenwart (present progressive)

- Wenn man sagen möchte, was gerade passiert, benutzt man die Verlaufsform der Gegenwart (*present progressive*).
- Die Verlaufsform bildet man so:

> Form von *be* (*am/is/are*) + Verb + *ing*

I	am	look**ing** for CDs.	Ich suche (gerade) nach CDs.
You	are	stand**ing** on my foot.	Du stehst (gerade) auf meinem Fuß.
He	is	wait**ing** for the guests.	Er wartet (gerade) auf die Gäste.
She	is	putt**ing** food on the table.	Sie stellt (gerade) Essen auf den Tisch.
It	is	rain**ing**.	Es regnet (gerade).
We	are	eat**ing** some cake.	Wir essen (gerade) Kuchen.
You	are	play**ing** football.	Ihr spielt (gerade) Fußball.
They	are	sitt**ing** on the sofa.	Sie sitzen (gerade) auf dem Sofa.